Praise for *Something Wonderful*

"By bringing children closer to nature—the complex nature of the tropics—this book both educates and delights! It is a joy for people of all ages to discover together."
—Peter H. Raven, U.S. National Medal of Science Recipient, Former President of the American Association for the Advancement of Science

"Wow! Matt and Nayl have hit a home run with this book. It will draw children deep into the web of life and help them discover the fascinating concept of mutualism!"
—Chipper Wichman, President, National Tropical Botanical Garden

"*Something Wonderful* helps our children understand the life history of strangling figs, the most impressive tropical rainforest trees. I can't imagine a better way to save these forests than to make children love them and all the organisms in them. Thank you, Matt Ritter and Nayl Gonzalez. And thank you to the frog!"
—Francis Hallé, author of Poetic Botany and In Praise of Plants, Professor, University of Montpellier, France

"From the first golden seed to the plop of the Chestnut-mandibled toucan's poop, this book shows the mysterious and intricate entwinements and cycles of a tropical rainforest."
—Sharon Lovejoy, author, illustrator, and recipient of the National Outdoor Book Award in Children's Literature

"This books tells complex stories of the rainforest in beautifully clear ways."
— Nalini M. Nadkarni, author of Between Earth and Sky: Our Intimate Connections to Trees, Professor, University of Utah

"An understanding of the natural world and what's in it is a source of not only a great curiosity but great fulfillment." — *Sir David Attenborough*

This book is dedicated to naturalist and broadcaster **Sir David Attenborough**, whose documentaries have opened the eyes of millions to the world's wonderful natural history.

Few people have done more to create a new generation of conservation biologists.

He has taught us all so much.

SOMETHING WONDERFUL

WRITTEN BY
MATT RITTER

ILLUSTRATED BY
NAYL GONZALEZ

PACIFIC ST.

PUBLISHING

In a hot and humid tropical forest,
on a day like any other...

...a golden seed fell
from the sky.

It was a fig seed, and it landed high
in the canopy of a giant tropical tree.

Something wonderful
was about to happen.

The seed settled
onto a branch
and did what
seeds do:
it germinated.

A tiny fig tree broke free from the seed coat and grew a slender, white root and two shiny, green leaves.

The small leaves grew
into larger leaves, each
stretching toward the sun.
The little fig's roots grew slowly.
They crawled downward along the
trunk of the giant tropical tree.

Eventually the roots
reached the forest floor.
They sucked water from the
soil, sending it to the leaves.
The fig began to grow quickly.

The years passed and the fig's
roots became thick and strong.

The powerful roots wove around
the tree's trunk. Although the
giant tree was strong
and had lived for many years,
it wasn't strong enough.

The roots were like steel cables,
strangling the old tree.
The giant couldn't grow any
wider and soon began to die.

Many years later, after the giant tree had died and rotted away, all that remained was a column of empty space inside the tangled web of fig roots.

Years passed and the fig grew stronger and larger.
It had taken the place of the giant tree in the forest.
Finally, the time had come for the fig to do what trees
do when they grow big: make more trees.

The fig tree made thousands of flowers,
hidden deep inside green globes.
Then it waited, but not for long.

A tiny mother wasp flying through the forest could smell the fig's hidden flowers. She'd come a long way through the forest and knew exactly what to do.

She found the best fig
and pushed her way
into a small hole
just her size.

Inside the fig
she moved around quickly,
laying her eggs and dusting
the fig flowers with pollen
she brought with her
from the fig
where she was born.

After all her eggs were
laid and all the flowers
were pollinated,
she rested.

She spent the rest of her life
inside the green fig
where baby wasps and
new fig seeds
were forming.

Her eggs soon began
to crack open.
When the baby wasps hatched,
they did what young wasps do:
they ate fig seeds.

And lots of them!

Young wasps ate the
nutritious seeds and
grew strong.

Females collected pollen
from the fig flowers.

Male wasps chewed escape holes
in the side of the fig.
Then the females unfolded
their delicate wings
and began their long journey
through the forest.

Like their mother had done before them,
each wasp flew off on a dangerous journey,
carrying pollen from the fig and hoping to catch
the scent of newly formed fig flowers
where each could lay her eggs.

Meanwhile, the green fig they
left behind became a ripe, yellow fig.
All the seeds that weren't eaten
turned golden while the fig ripened
around them. The figs were ready,
and they didn't wait long.

Something wonderful
was about to happen.

A chestnut-mandibled toucan flew through the forest and saw thousands of ripe figs on the tree.

Ripe figs are
a chestnut-mandibled
toucan's favorite food.

She ate as many figs as she could,
then ate some more,
until she couldn't fit another fig
in her beak.

When she was full,
she began her long flight
back to her nest.
On her way, she did what
toucans do:
she pooped.

One of the golden seeds
from her poop
landed on a branch
high in the canopy of
a giant tropical tree.
The seed settled on the branch,
and did what seeds do:
it germinated.

DID YOU FIND ME?

The lifecycle of fig wasps is interconnected with the lifecycle of the fig trees they inhabit.

1 A female fig wasp (Agaonidae) carrying pollen and her fertilized eggs crawls inside an unripe fig. A fig is a chamber full of flowers with only a small opening on one end. On her way in she often loses her wings and antennas.

2 She deposits pollen from a different fig tree onto the female flowers. She then lays her eggs inside some of the flowers.

The female wasp then dies inside the fig she has just pollinated.

3 Male wasps hatch and fertilize the eggs of new female wasps while they are still inside their flowers. The males then chew tunnels in the fig's wall through which fertilized females can escape.

Then the male wasps die without ever leaving the fig.

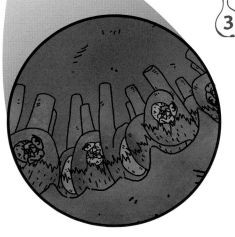

4 The fertilized females eventually hatch from their flowers and, while moving around inside the fig, collect pollen from the fig's male flowers.

5 Once they have all the pollen they can carry, females escape through the tunnels chewed open by the males. Female wasps take flight, searching for another unripe fig so their lifecycle can begin again.

After female pollinating wasps leave, the fig ripens, turning bright yellow, orange, or black, and the seeds inside become mature. Many different animals in the forest eat ripe figs and disperse the seeds inside when they poop, leaving behind fig seeds to germinate in a pile of fertilizer.

Red-Eyed Tree Frog
Agalychnis callidryas

Red-eyed tree frogs live in the lowland rainforests of southern Mexico, Central America, and south to Columbia. They spend their lives in trees and are excellent climbers and jumpers. Their webbed toes are red and orange, each with a sticky pad on the bottom that allows them to cling to slippery, wet leaves. Red-eyed tree frogs blend in with their leafy environment by closing their eyes, tucking their feet, and hiding their blue sides with their legs. If a predator approaches, they can open their bulging red eyes, startling the predator and allowing them to escape. They hunt at night, eating all kinds of insects and occasionally smaller frogs. Depending on their mood, they can change color from lime green to dark green or reddish-brown.

Red-eyed tree frogs are amphibians. Many of the world's amphibians, such as frogs, toads, newts, and salamanders, have declined in abundance in recent years. The red-eyed tree frog is not endangered, but its tropical rainforest home is constantly threatened.

There are over
800 different species of
fig trees in the world, most
living in tropical rainforests. They
are all in the same genus: *Ficus*. One of
these species, the edible fig, *Ficus carica*,
is widely grown for its delicious fruit.
Each fig species is pollinated by its own
specialized type of wasp that evolved along
with the tree. Humans have had a long
relationship with figs, which have been
a source of shade, food, medicine,
building materials, and...

Chestnut-Mandibled Toucan
Ramphastos swainsonii

Chestnut-mandibled toucans live in Central America and northern South America, usually in moist lowland forests, where they are the largest of all the toucans. They are primarily fruit eaters, but will occasionally eat insects, lizards, frogs, and the eggs of other birds. They travel in small flocks from treetop to treetop, calling to each other in piercing yelps from their perches. Chestnut-mandible toucans lay their eggs high up in the canopy in small openings of dead or dying parts of tall trees. Both parents sit on the eggs, and once they hatch, they both take turns feeding the young chicks. After six weeks, the young toucans learn to fly, then they leave the nest but continue to get help from the parents for some time. These large and colorful birds play a crucial ecological role by dispersing the seeds of many types of trees, including figs!

Thank You

Sam Baber, Abel, May, and Sarah Ritter, Jim Mauseth, Dave Keil, Ed Himelblau, Enrica Lovaglio Costello, Dean Nicolle, Annett Boerner, Ivan, Oliver, and Imojean Gonzalez, Nora Bales, Jazzmyne Parker, Fiona Carlsen, and Jenn Yost.

Published by Pacific Street Publishing

ISBN: 978-0-9998960-1-3
Library of Congress Control Number: 2019950501

Hand lettering by Sam Baber
Book layout and design by Matt Ritter and Sam Baber

Orders, inquiries, and correspondence should be addressed to:
Pacific Street Publishing
San Luis Obispo, California
www.pacificstreetpublishing.com

Manufactured in China by Artron Printing America, Inc.

10 9 8 7 6 5 4 3 2

FSC
www.fsc.org
MIX
Paper from
responsible sources
FSC® C019910